Primarily Logic

Written by
Judy Leimbach

Illustrated by
Dean and **Pat Crawford**

PRUFROCK PRESS INC.

Prince George's County Public Schools
TAG Program

Edited by Dianne Draze

ISBN-10: 1-59363-122-7
ISBN-13: 978-1-59363-122-2

Prufrock Press, Inc.
P.O. Box 8813
Waco, Texas 76714-8813
(800) 998-2208
Fax (800) 240-0333
http://www.prufrock.com

Contents

Instructions for Teachers

Finding Relationships and Group Membership - Analyzing Groups for Shared Relationships

Lesson 1 - This worksheet may be used as a group lesson to introduce the concepts of group membership and shared relationships.

Lesson 2 - Follow-up for individual practice.

Lesson 3 - This worksheet should be done individually and then discussed. Answers will vary. Students should give their answers and explain the relationships they see.

Related Activity - Categories Games
    (1) Leader names a category. Players take turns naming members of the category.
    (2) Leader names things that belong to a category and players try to name the category.
    Some ideas - Things that are yellow, round, rubber.
                Things that have zippers, drawers, feet.
                Things that you see at a birthday party, say on the phone, hear at the circus.

Lessons 4 and 5 - Use the example at the top of the page to explain that some members within a category may share certain relationships, making up a subset within the larger group.

For example:
Nickel, dime, dollar, quarter, and penny are all money; but if you take out the dollar, the remaining four are all coins.

You may put other examples on the board. An additional example might be cake, cookies, candy, lemons, and jam are foods; but if you take out the lemons, the four remaining are sweet.

Students must be able to explain why a particular word is removed by pointing out the **relationship between the remaining words,** not "I took out the lemon because it is the only fruit."

These worksheets can be done individually and then discussed. Answers may vary. A creative student may see some other relationships than the obvious ones.

Related Activity - Ms. Mystery Game
    The leader decides what category of things Ms. Mystery likes, then begins naming things she likes and things she doesn't like. Players try to determine the shared relationship of the things she likes. When players think they know, they can test their theories by asking the leader if Ms. Mystery likes a certain thing.
    For example: The leader decides Ms. Mystery likes black things.
    Leader: Ms. Mystery likes licorice, but doesn't like chocolate. Ms. Mystery likes witch's hats, but not their brooms. Ms. Mystery likes (something black in the room) but doesn't like (something else in the room.) Etc.
    Player 1: Does Ms. Mystery like chalk?
    Leader: No!
    Player 2: Does Ms. Mystery like charcoal?
    Leader: Yes!
    Play continues until everyone sees the relationship between the things Ms. Mystery likes. Some ideas for Ms. Mystery: things in a classroom, kids with striped shirts, things that start with S, things with double letters.

Analogous Relationships - Looking for relationships between words based on shared characteristics.

Lesson 6 - Varied relationships. This page is an introduction to the section on analogous relationships, because it demonstrates that words can be related in a variety of ways.

Use the top of this page to explain that although "fishing" and "telephone" are not related, they are both related to "pole." You may want to put other examples on the board to discuss. Examples: bean, golf (green)
sleeping, mark (beauty)
bow, drop (rain)
light, time (day)
light, shine (sun)

Lesson 7 - Practice in analyzing relationships based on non-obvious, shared characteristics.

Lesson 8 - Group lesson to teach the meaning of analogies and introduce one type of analogy based on characteristics.

Lessons 9 - 13 - Introduce students to a variety of analogous relationships: characteristic, part-to-whole, member of category, actions, synonyms, and antonyms.

Lessons 14 and 15 - Provide practice in completing analogies covering a variety of relationships.

Lesson 16 - Provide practice in supplying the second pair of words to complete analogies.

Related Activity - Individual applications
Students write their own analogies.
Discuss analogous relationships in real life, literature, etc. Point out a relationship and ask for similar relationships.

Deductive Reasoning - Logical Reasoning and Using All Statements

Lesson 17 - Group lesson to introduce all statements.

Lessons 18 - 19 - Group lessons introducing logical reasoning and the rule of logic regarding "all" statements.

Lesson 20 - Individual practice applying rules of logic to "all" statements.

Lesson 21 - Group lesson demonstrating some statements imply "all" and are treated as "all" statements in logical reasoning, and whether stated or implied, you cannot reverse "all" statements.

Lesson 22 - Group lesson teaching rule of logic regarding "no" statements.

Lesson 23 - Individual practice applying rules of logic to "no" statements.

Lesson 24 - Group lesson demonstrating some statements imply "no" and are treated as "no" statements in logical reasoning.

Lesson 25 - Individual practice applying rules of logic when reversing statements.

Lesson 26 - Group lesson introducing syllogisms and validity.

Lessons 27 and 28 - Individual practice in determining whether syllogisms are valid or invalid.

Lesson 29 - Group lesson introducing rule of logic regarding "if, then" statements.

Lesson 30 - Individual practice applying rules of logic to "if, then" statements.

Related Activity - Individual application
Students give examples of "all," "no," and "if, then" statements. Test rules of logic by reversing them and seeing if they are still true.

Problem Solving, Deductive Reasoning, and Organizing Information

Lessons 31 and 32 - Group lessons to teach how to use the grid to organize information. Go through each problem together and discuss strategy.

The first example might follow these lines. From the statement "Sally's story did not have a wolf in it," students can conclude she did not read "The Three Little Pigs" or "Red Riding Hood." Students write "no" or mark an "O" in appropriate boxes on the grid. Therefore, Sally read "The Three Bears." Students write "yes" or mark an "X" in the box showing Sally read "The Three Bears" and "no" or "O" showing Bob and Jim did not read "The Three Bears."

Complete charts in this manner.

	Bob	Sally	Jimmy
The Three Bears	O	x	O
Three Little Pigs			x
Little Red Riding Hood	x		

With primary-age students it is less confusing to start with "no" and "yes." It is an easy transition later on to drop the "N" and just put "O" and "X" for "yes".

Lessons 33 - 36 Individual practice in using charts to organize information and reach conclusions.

Lesson 37 - This lesson may be used to demonstrate an additional method of organizing information. When problems contain clues referring to more or less, higher or lower, before or after, etc. it may be helpful to make a mini-chart showing this information.

For example: Clue 2 tells us "Brian collected more than both girls and Phil, but less than Tim."
This information can be shown in this way: Tim
Brian
Karen-Megan-Phil
By looking at this hierarchy students can easily conclude that Tim had the most (100) and Brian was next (95).

Lessons 38-40 Individual practice in organizing information including greater, lesser or chronological order.

Lessons 41 and 42 - Extra challenge (using double chart) for those students who are ready to try more difficult problems.

Related Activity - Creating Logic Puzzles

Have students write their own logic puzzles.

First try working as a group to write some puzzles on the board.

First, decide on categories—what things will be matched in your puzzle (first and last names, names and favorite foods, etc.).

Next, decide on names. Then draw a chart on the board and fill in the things to be matched and the answers.

Finally, as students suggest clues, write them on the board and fill the chart in with all the information which can be deducted from each clue. Continue until all items in the puzzle have been matched up.

When students clearly understand the process, individual students may want to create their own logic puzzles for their classmates to solve.

Four of a Kind

Name_____

Look carefully at the four items in each group. Decide what the relationship is for each group. On the line, write how the four things are related.

1. cup, plate, saucer, platter - _____

2. pork chops, hamburger, hot dogs, bacon - _____

3. red, blue, yellow, green - _____

4. tea, milk, coffee, lemonade - _____

5. robin, cardinal, blue jay, sparrow - _____

6. daisy, tulip, rose, petunia - _____

7. cake, cookies, pie, ice cream - _____

8. piano, guitar, trumpet, clarinet - _____

9. table, chair, sofa, desk - _____

10. blouse, shirt, jacket, skirt - _____

11. north, south, east, west - _____

12. California, Illinois, Florida, Colorado - _____

13. Snow White, Cinderella, Tom Thumb, Pinocchio - _____

Missing Link

Name_____

Each of the words in the box is related to one group of words below. Write each word from the box under the group where it belongs.

_____ Word Box _____

Chicago	frog	saw
skip	John	snow
flashlight	scared	mittens
flower	Lori	basketball

1. baseball football soccer _____	2. Jimmy Brad Richard _____	3. hammer screwdriver chisel _____
4. torch lamp candle _____	5. tree bush grass _____	6. New York Boston Miami _____
7. Jane Heather Erin _____	8. happy surprised sad _____	9. sunshine rain fog _____
10. grass dollars shamrock _____	11. run jump hop _____	12. shoes socks gloves _____

Creating Relations

Name_____

Decide in what way the words in each group go together. Add another word that is related in the same way.

1. pencil   crayon   chalk _____

2. gerbil   kitten   parakeet _____

3. pine   oak   maple _____

4. lemon   lime   grapefruit _____

5. banana   ice cream   whipped cream _____

6. trunk   branch   root _____

7. touch   taste   smell _____

8. basket   bucket   jar _____

9. sunshine   rain   fog _____

10. 4th of July   Halloween   Christmas _____

11. rose   catsup   blood _____

12. gym   art   music _____

13

Take It Out

Name_____

Which member of this group does not belong?

nickel   dime   dollar

quarter   penny

Look at each group of words. Decide which one in each group does not belong. Write the one word that does not belong. Then tell in what way the remaining four are related.

1. ladybug, beetle, canary, grasshopper, cricket

Take out _____   The rest are _____

2. wheel, pedal, seat, skate, handle bars

Take out _____   The rest are _____

3. carrots, cherries, beans, broccoli, peas

Take out _____   The rest are _____

4. tiger, bear, lion, kitten, wolf

Take out _____   The rest are _____

5. car, truck, boat, bicycle, wagon

Take out _____   The rest _____

6. school, teacher, student, mother, father

Take out _____   The rest are _____

7. tiny, little, big, small, wee

Take out _____   The rest are _____

8. belt, hat, sunglasses, earrings, earmuffs

Take out _____   The rest are _____

9. hammer, wrench, shovel, screw driver, pliers

Take out _____   The rest are _____

14

Looking for Relationships

Name _____

In each box you will find a group of pictures or symbols. Cross out the one that does not belong. In what ways are the ones that remain related? Write the way they are related on the line.

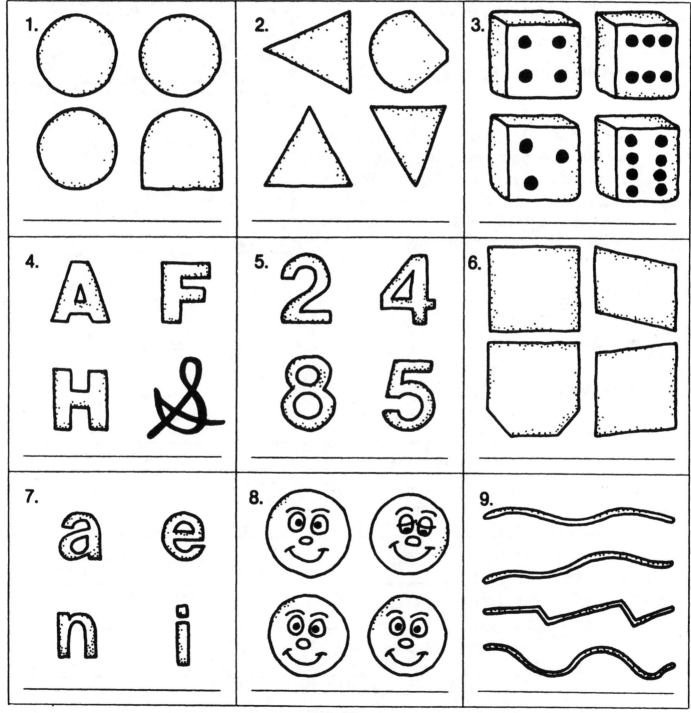

© Prufrock Press Inc - Primarily Logic

Curious Connections

Name_____

In this lesson, you will be looking for relationships between two things that are not obvious. Both words in each pair are related to a third word, but they are not related to each other.

For example:

fishing and **telephone** are

related to **pole**

fishing pole and **telephone pole**

Look at each pair of words. Then decide how each word is related to one of the four words listed below the pair of words. Select the word that is related to **both** words in the problem. Write that word on the line.

1. duster, bird   _____

   fluffy, hen, feather, dirt

2. bone, fish   _____

   dog, white, swim, hard

3. mark, worm   _____

   scribble, wiggle, book, hand

4. bon, fly   _____

   candy, high, good, fire

5. back, china   _____

   break, bone, spine, white

6. jay, jeans   _____

   pants, bird, blue, cat

7. board, bird   _____

   black, dark, fly, wood

8. day, stone   _____

   night, rock, shelf, birth

9. base, foot   _____

   hand, bottom, ball, round

16

Being a Detective

Name_____

This exercise will require that you think like a detective. You must be clever and look beyond the obvious. Each pair of words below is not necessarily related to each other. But each word is related to one of the words in the word box. Write each word from the word box on one of the lines below. Remember that the word you choose must be related in some way to both of the words in the pair.

Word Box

| ball | blue | bow | plant | fly | park | right | bed | cow |

1. sad   sky   _____

2. plane   mosquito   _____

3. bat   snow   _____

4. boy   hide   _____

5. left   correct   _____

6. ribbon   rain   _____

7. bug   rest   _____

8. seeds   factory   _____

9. car   playground   _____

17

Cuing Into Characteristics

Name_____

Analogies are special kinds of puzzles. An **analogy** makes a comparison between two different sets of things. To solve the puzzles you need to think about how the words are related.

For example:

We say: **Apple is to red as lemon is to yellow.**

Other examples are:
   Leaves are to green as bark is to brown.
   Paper is to thin as cardboard is to thick.
   Knife is to sharp as spoon is to rounded.

These are examples of a **characteristic analogy**. One of the words describes a characteristic or attribute of the other word.

Look for the relationship between the first pair of words. Use the words in the word box to fill in the blanks so that there will be the same relationship between the second pair of words.

_____ **Word Box** _____

night	green	rough	small
round	turtle	strong	furry

1. Elephant is to big as ant is to _____

2. Box is to square as ball is to _____

3. Roses are red as grass is to _____

4. Baby is to weak as Superman is to _____

5. Light is to day as dark is to _____

6. Swift is to deer as slow is to _____

7. Glass is to smooth as sandpaper is to _____

8. Fish is to scaly as bear is to _____

18

Rhyming Analogies

Name_____

"Roses are red, violets are blue,
Sugar is sweet..."

Charley is tired of these old, worn-out descriptions. He is looking for new characteristic combinations for poems and riddles. He has thought of the first two words for each pair, but he needs some help completing the second pair. Write a word that completes each characteristic analogy.

1. Roses are to red as corn is to _____

   Soft is to whisper as loud is to _____

2. Brown is to lizard and green is to _____

   Meow is to cat as bark is to _____

3. Cold is to ice as hot is to _____

   Athletic is to team as musical is to _____

4. Mud is to brown as snow is to _____

   Rock is to heavy as feather is to _____

5. Lemon is to sour as candy is to _____

   Blue is to blue jay as green is to _____

6. Rich is to wealthy as penniless is to _____

   Bee is to buzz as frog is to _____

Word Box

broke	bellow	dog	fire
sweet	croak	white	light
yellow	frog	choir	parakeet

19

Picking Parts

Name_____

The analogies in this exercise are called **part-to-whole** analogies. One word in each pair is a part of the other word.

Example:

String is to violin as core is to apple.

Eraser is to pencil as lace is to shoe.

Look for the relationship between the first pair of words. Choose a word to fill in the blank so the same relationship fits the second pair of words.

1. Feathers are to birds as fur is to _____

              coat   warm   bear

2. Buckle is to belt as laces are to _____

              shoes   tie   bow

3. Toes are to foot as fingers are to _____

              nails   hand   toes

4. Hand is to arm as foot is to _____

              walk   toes   leg

5. Cherries are to pie as chocolate chips are to _____

              cookies   bake   sweet

6. Goal posts are to football field as homeplate is to _____

              batter   home run   baseball diamond

7. Runners are to ice skates as wheels are to _____

              round   roller skates   train

8. Bird is to beak as dog is to _____

              tail   bark   mouth

9. Window is to glass as house is to _____

              home   bricks   door

10. Grass is to blade as flower is to _____

              petal   roots   roses

Mainly Members

Name_____

In these analogies, one word in each pair is
a member of a group named by the other word.

Example:
   Cow is to herd as sheep is to flock.
   Note is to song as word is to story.
   Horse is to mammal as ladybug is to insect.

Look at the first two words in each puzzle. Then find a word that completes
the second pair of words.

Word Box

dog	tree	rocky road	fruit
fish	Ben	animal	chair
figures	Ohio	ham	cereal

1. Carrot is to vegetable as apple is to _____.

2. Elephant is to mammal as tuna is to _____.

3. Hammer is to tool as _____ is to furniture.

4. Chicken noodle is to soup as _____ is to ice cream.

5. Sara is to girls' names as _____ is to boys' names.

6. Siamese is to cat as collie is to _____.

7. Red is to colors as triangle is to _____.

8. Chicago is to city as _____ is to state.

9. Shirt is to clothes as _____ is to food.

10. Tree is to plant as giraffe is to _____.

11. Pork is to meat as oatmeal is to _____.

12. Tulip is to flower as oak is to_____.

Ready, Set, Action

Name_____

The puzzles on this page are **action analogies**. Each pair of words contains a thing and an action that is related to this thing.

Example:

Fly is to plane as sail is to boat.
Snake is to slither as fish is to swim.
Beak is to peck as wing is to fly.

Read each pair of words in the first part of each problem. Then choose the best word to complete the second part of the analogy.

1. Whale is to swim as eagle is to _____.

| bird | fly | wings |

2. Saw is to cut as hammer is to _____.

| wood | tool | pound |

3. Ball is to throw as bat is to _____.

| wood | hit | game |

4. Milk is to drink as bread is to _____.

| eat | sandwich | butter |

5. Hands are to clap as feet are to _____.

| toes | shoes | tap |

6. Crayon is to draw as pencil is to _____.

| paper | write | lead |

7. Game is to play as bicycle is to _____.

| wheels | toy | ride |

8. Kangaroo is to hop as dog is to _____.

| run | bark | puppy |

9. Teacher is to teach as student is to _____.

| school | learn | child |

10. Cat is to purr as bird is to _____.

| fly | nest | chirp |

Similar or Opposite

Name_____

This page has analogies that are either similar (synonyms) or opposite (antonyms). To solve these problems, you have to decide if the words in the first part of the analogy are similar or opposite. Then you have to find a word to complete the second pair of the analogy in the same way.

Example:
Synonym (similar)
Small is to tiny as large is to big.
Yell is to shout as twelve is to dozen.
Antonym (opposite)
Small is to large as thin is to thick.
Sharp is to dull as smooth is to rough.

Look at each problem. Decide if the first part of the analogy is showing two things that are similar or opposite. Find a word to complete the second part of the analogy in the same way.

1. Sun is to moon as day is to _____.

          today   night   afternoon

2. Big is to little as large is to _____.

          small   huge   giant

3. Big is to huge as little is to _____.

          large   overgrown   tiny

4. Happy is to glad as unhappy is to _____.

          tears   sad   overjoyed

5. Right is to wrong as good is to _____.

          bad   correct   night

6. Up is to high as down is to _____.

          under   over   low

7. Mad is to angry as frightened is to _____.

          happy   brave   scared

8. Dog is to puppy as cat is to _____.

          kitten   mammal   animal

9. Woman is to man as girl is to _____.

          child   lady   boy

10. Hot is to warm as cold is to _____.

          heat   cool   ice

Analogies, Anyone?

Name _____

Here's a review of all of the different kinds of analogies that you have learned to solve so far. Look carefully at the first two words in each problem. Once you have discovered how the two words are related, select a word that completes the second part of the analogy in the same manner. In each case, choose the **best** word to complete each analogy.

1. Entrance is to exit as basement is to _____.
        attic   house   cellar

2. Puddle is to pond as dinner is to _____.
       breakfast   plate   banquet

3. Furious is to angry as overjoyed is to _____.
        happy   surprised   sad

4. Alarm is to warn as filter is to _____.
       cigarette   furnace   clean

5. Bacon is to fry as cake is to _____.
        frost   bake   eat

6. Orchestra is to conductor as team is to _____.
       player   football   coach

7. Speak is to microphone as look is to _____.
       picture   microscope   vision

8. Cobra is to reptile as whale is to _____.
        fish   ocean   mammal

9. Read is to words as play is to _____.
       dance   notes   book

10. Catch is to throw as tell is to _____.
        hear   speak   ball

11. Trout is to fish as ant is to _____.
       small   fly   insect

12. Lumber is to house as pages are to _____.
       paper   book   numbers

13. Yellow is to lemon as prickly is to _____.
      porcupine   lime   smooth

Analogy Round Up

Name_____

Sidekick Sam has rounded up a collection of different kinds of analogy puzzles. He's better at rounding up than he is at solving, so he needs your help. Look carefully at each problem. Decide what kind of relationship exists between the first two words. Then find a word that completes the second part of the analogy in the same way.

Word Box

read	hammer	club	fly	cricket
eat	library	scissors	paper	house
land	cereal	bark	person	nervous

1. Artist is to brush as carpenter is to _____.

2. Bird is to nest as child is to _____.

3. Fish is to swim as bird is to _____.

4. Reptile is to snake as insect is to _____.

5. Plane is to sky as car is to _____.

6. Baseball is to bat as golf is to _____.

7. Chalk is to chalkboard as pencil is to _____.

8. Milk is to drink as bread is to _____.

9. Grass is to lawnmower as hair is to _____.

10. Steak is to meat as oatmeal is to _____.

11. Man is to talk as dog is to _____.

12. Music is to play as books are to _____.

13. Happy is to joyful as tense is to _____.

14. Crawl is to worm as walk is to _____.

15. Cakes are to bakery as books are to _____.

25

Creating Analogies

Name_____

Here's your chance to create you own analogies. Read the first part of the analogy in each problem. Decide what the relationship is between the two words. Use that relationship to choose two words to complete the analogy.

PIG is to Oink as

1. Pig is to oink as _____ is to _____

2. Empty is to full as _____ is to _____.

3. Scales are to fish as _____ is to _____.

4. Car is to drive as _____ is to _____.

5. Sun is to day as _____ is to _____.

6. Jet is to fast as _____ is to _____.

7. Car is to tire as _____ is to _____.

8. Chair is to furniture as _____ is to _____.

9. Happy is to sad as _____ is to _____.

10. Girl is to Megan as _____ is to _____.

11. Listen is to records as _____ is to _____.

12. Fire is to hot as _____ is to _____.

26

All Together

Name_____

An **all statement** is a statement that is true for all members of a group. Also if it is true for the group as a whole, it is true for all members of the group.

Example:
All fruits have seeds.
A cherry is a fruit.
So we know **a cherry has seeds.**

An apple is a fruit.
So we know an apple _____.

An orange is fruit.
So we know an orange _____.

A banana is fruit.
Does a banana have seeds? _____
   (Even very tiny seeds count!!)

Use what you have just learned about **all statements** to complete these statements.

1. All dogs were once puppies.
   Fido is a dog.
   We know that Fido _____.

2. All vowels are part of the alphabet.
   "E" is a vowel.
   We know that "E" _____.

3. All squares have four sides.
   Myra's drawing is in the shape of a square.
   We know that Myra's drawing _____.

4. All even numbers are divisible by two.
   1028 is an even number.
   We know that 1028 _____.

5. All cars have wheels.
   My Ford is a car.
   We know that my Ford _____.

Using All Statements

Name _____

Now that you can recognize **all statements**, we will combine them with another kind of statement called an **if statement**. If the first two parts of the statement are true, then the third part should also be true.

Example:
   If all cats like fish and **Puff is a cat**, then we know that **Puff likes fish.**

Read these statements and answer the questions. For the last three, complete the "then" part of the statement.

1. If it is true all birds lay eggs, and an ostrich is a bird, does an ostrich lay eggs? _____

2. If it is true all insects have six legs, and a katydid is an insect, how many legs does a katydid have? _____

3. If it is true all reptiles are cold-blooded, and a snake is a reptile, is a snake cold-blooded? _____

4. If it is true all blonks are green, and a flub is a blonk, what color is a flub?

   _____

5. If it is true all zippies are fast, and a node is a zippy, is a node fast? _____

6. If it is true all children are special, and you are a child, are you special?_____

7. If all schools need teachers and Mt. Washington is a school, then _____

   _____

8. If all candy is sweet, and Snickers is a candy, then _____

   _____

9. If all bears have fur, and a grizzly is a bear, then _____

Logic in Reverse

Name_____

You have learned how to draw conclusions using **all statements**. But if you turn these statements around, will they still be true?

Example:
All dogs can bark.
A poodle is a dog.
So a poodle can bark.
But can you say that **all things that bark are dogs?**
Seals bark. Does this mean all seals are dogs? Of course not.
Just because all dogs can bark, does not mean everything that barks is a dog!

 You cannot reverse an "all statement."

Read these statements and tell whether they are true or not.

1. All zebras are striped.
   Zeke is our pet zebra.
   Is Zeke striped? _____
   My shirt is striped.
   Does this mean my shirt is a zebra? _____

2. All fish can swim.
   A trout is a fish.
   Can a trout swim? _____
   I can swim.
   Does this mean I am a fish? _____

3. All carrots are vegetables.
   I have a carrot in my lunch.
   Do I have a vegetable in my lunch? _____
   A bean is a vegetable.
   Does this mean a bean is a carrot? _____

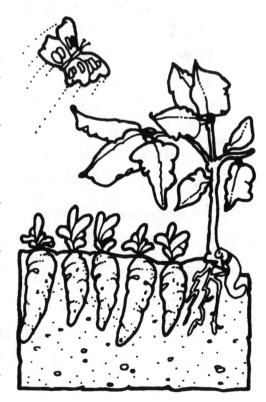

29

Reversals in Review

Name_____

Here is some more practice with **all statements** and their reversals. Read each statement carefully and answer "yes" or "no."

1. If it is true that all apples are fruits, does that mean all fruits are apples? ____

2. If it is true that all turtles have shells, does that mean everything with a shell is a turtle? _____

3. If it is true that all dollar bills are green, does that mean all green things are dollar bills? _____

4. All horses have four legs. Is everything with four legs a horse? _____

5. All cats have fur.
   Patches is a cat.
   Does Patches have fur? _____
   My mink coat has fur.
   Is my mink coat a cat? _____

6. All cars have wheels.
   A Chevy is a car.
   Does a Chevy have wheels? _____
   A bicycle has wheels.
   Is a bicycle a car? _____

7. All fruits have seeds.
   A cucumber has seeds.
   Is a cucumber a fruit? _____
   A watermelon is a fruit.
   Does a watermelon have seeds? _____

8. All beanies are blue.

   Are all blue things beanies? _____

   Are any beanies not blue? _____

   If a zoop is a beanie, is a zoop blue? _____

   If a zip is not a beanie could a zip be blue? _____

   Some crayons are blue. Does that mean they're beanies? _____

DO I HAVE TWO OR FOUR LEGS?

30

The Unstated All

Name_____

Sometimes statements don't say **all** but they mean **all**.

Example:

Dinosaurs are extinct means **all** dinosaurs.

Tigers belong to the cat family means **all** tigers.

Wheels are round means **all** wheels.

Read these statements carefully. Then answer the question that follows the statement.

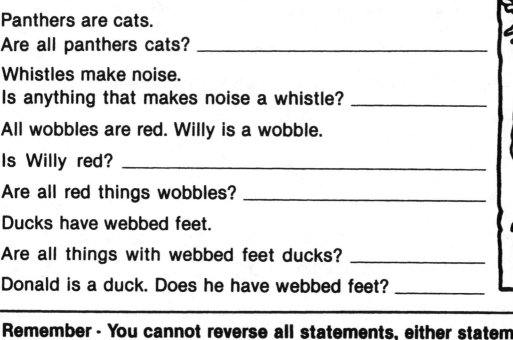

1. Shoes are worn on feet.
   Are all shoes worn on feet? _____

2. All squares are rectangles.
   Are all rectangles squares? _____

3. Grasshoppers are insects.
   Are all insects grasshoppers? _____

4. Robins can fly.
   Are things that can fly always robins? _____

5. Panthers are cats.
   Are all panthers cats? _____

6. Whistles make noise.
   Is anything that makes noise a whistle? _____

7. All wobbles are red. Willy is a wobble.

   Is Willy red? _____

   Are all red things wobbles? _____

8. Ducks have webbed feet.

   Are all things with webbed feet ducks? _____

   Donald is a duck. Does he have webbed feet? _____

Remember - You cannot reverse all statements, either statements that begin with "all" or imply all.

Introducing No Statements

Name_____

No statements are different from **all statements** in two important ways. **No statements** begin with the word "no" instead of the word "all." Also **no statements** can be reversed and still be true.

Example:
If it is true that **no giraffes are birds**, then it must also be true that **no birds are giraffes.**
If there was just one little bird that was a giraffe, then it would not be true that no giraffes are birds!

Read these **no statements**. Answer the question that follows each statement.

1. If no bicycles are cars, can any cars be bicycles? _____

   Why? _____

2. If no cars have wings, can anything with wings be a car? _____

   Why? _____

3. If no cars can swim, can anything that can swims be a car? _____

   Why? _____

Write the reverse of each of these **no statements**.

4. No mammals have feathers, and no animals with feathers _____

   _____

5. No rabbits are purple, and no purple things _____

6. If no dogs are cats, then no cats _____

7. If no gleeks are glops, then no _____

32

Tricky Truths

Name_____

Here are some **no statements**. Read the
pairs of statements in each problem. You
may assume that the first statement in each
pair is true. Decide if the second statement
in each pair is also true. Write "true" or "false" on the line.

1. No frogs are tennis players.

   No tennis players are frogs _____

2. No lions are tame.

   No tame animals are lions. _____

3. No aliens have antennas.

   Nothing with antennas is an alien. _____

4. No witches are pretty.

   Only a few pretty girls are witches. _____

5. No bloops are wimmers.

   No wimmers are bloops. _____

6. No heebies are purple.

   Only small purple things are heebies. _____

7. No klids are animals.

   Only some animals may be klids. _____

8. No children own cars.

   A few car-owners are children. _____

9. No sweets are sour.

   Sour things are not sweet._____

Write your own **no statements** and a reversal for each statement.

10. _____

    _____

11. _____

    _____

33

No and Other Negatives

Name_____

Sometimes statements don't say "no," but they mean "no." There are several ways of making a **no statement** without actually using the word "no."

Example:
   Tigers do not have wings means **no tigers have wings.**

   Penguins can't fly means **no penguins fly.**

Remember that you can reverse a **no statement** whether the statement begins with the word "no" or no is implied.

Read the following pairs of statements. You may assume that the first statement in each pair is true. Decide if the second statement is also true. Write true or false on the line.

1. Frogs are not purple.
   No purple things are frogs. _____

2. Elephants can't sing.
   Singers are not elephants. _____

3. Nothing that flies is a walrus.
   No walrus can fly. _____

4. Balloons do not eat peanuts.
   Nothing that eats peanuts is a balloon. _____

Write the reverse of each of the following statements.

5. Nothing with fur flies.

   _____

6. Green things don't taste good.

   _____

7. Turkeys are not smart.

   _____

34

Put It In Reverse

Name_____

Read each pair of statements carefully. You may assume the first statement is true. Can you correctly assume the second statement is true? Write "true" or "false" on the line next to each pair of statements.

1. All elephants have trunks.

   Therefore, everything with a trunk is an elephant. _____

2. No mice are elephants.

   Therefore, no elephants are mice. _____

3. All collies are dogs.

   Therefore, all dogs are collies. _____

4. No aliens are earthmen.

   Therefore, no earthmen are aliens. _____

5. No weezers are striped.

   Therefore, no striped things are weezers. _____

6. All blonks are beneath the sea.

   Therefore, everything beneath the sea is a blonk. _____

7. Nothing with hair is a baldino.

   Therefore, no baldinoes have hair. _____

8. Creepies are frightening.

   Therefore, all frightening things are creepies. _____

9. All dogs have four legs.

   Therefore, all things with four legs are dogs. _____

10. No fish can talk.

    Therefore, nothing that talks is a fish. _____

11. All fish can swim.

    Therefore, all things that swim are fish. _____

35

Introducing Syllogisms

> A **syllogism** is made up of three statements. The first two statements are the *premises*. The third statement is the *conclusion.* Premises may be **all statements** or **no statements**. If a conclusion can be supported by the two premises, then it is true or valid. If a conclusion cannot be supported by the two premises, then it is false or invalid. We assume that the first two statements (premises) are true and try to decide if they prove the conclusion.

Example 1:
All insects are six-legged creatures. (premise 1)
All beetles are insects. (premise 2)
Therefore, all beetles are six-legged creatures. (conclusion)

This is a *valid* conclusion. If all beetles are insects as stated in statement 2, then they must have six legs as stated in statement 1.

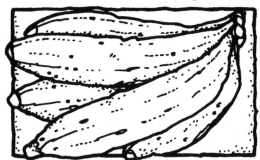

Example 2:
All bananas are fruits. (premise 1)
All bananas are yellow. (premise 2)
Therefore, all fruits are yellow. (conclusion)

This is an *invalid* conclusion. We do not have any proof that all fruits are yellow. Just because bananas are yellow and they are fruits, it does not follow that all fruits are yellow. Remember, you cannot reverse an "all statement." All bananas are fruits cannot be reversed to mean all fruits are bananas.

Example 3:
All daisies are flowers.
No flowers are ugly.
Therefore, no daisies are ugly.

This is a *valid* conclusion.
If no flowers are ugly (second statement) then no daisies are ugly, because they are flowers (first statement).

36

Syllogism Sampling

Name _____

Each problem includes two statements and a conclusion. Read each statement carefully. Then decide if the conclusion is valid or invalid. Write "valid" or "invalid" on the line.

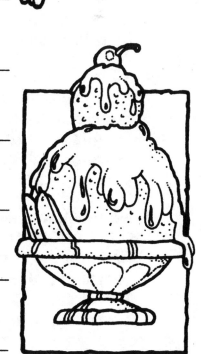

1. All monkeys have long tails.
   All marmosets are monkeys.
   Therefore, all marmosets have long tails. _____

2. All cobras are snakes.
   All cobras are poisonous.
   Therefore, all snakes are poisonous. _____

3. All quartz are minerals.
   No minerals are plants.
   Therefore, no quartz are plants. _____

4. All dragons are scaly.
   No scarabs are scaly.
   Therefore, no scarabs are dragons. _____

5. All trumpos are fleebs.
   All trumpos are brass.
   Therefore, all fleebs are brass. _____

6. No fruits are vegetables.
   All apples are fruits.
   Therefore, no apples are vegetables. _____

7. All candies are sweet.
   No sweet things are sour.
   Therefore, no candies are sour. _____

8. All wheels are round.
   All round things can roll.
   Therefore, wheels can roll. _____

9. No glots are green.
   All strams are glots.
   Therefore, no strams are green. _____

10. All unos are lups.
    All lups are single.
    Therefore, all unos are single. _____

Syllogism Scrimmage

Name_____

Each problem includes two statements (or premises) and several conclusions. You can assume that the statements are true. Read the statements carefully. Then decide which of the conclusions are supported by the statements. Answer each question "yes" or "no."

1. All redheads are smart.
   Shelly has red hair.
   Can you conclude:
   Therefore, Shelly is smart? _____
   Therefore, all smart people are redheads? _____
   Therefore, all redheads are named Shelly? _____

2. All soccer players are brave.
   Sam is a soccer player.
   Can you conclude:
   Therefore, all brave people are soccer players? _____
   Therefore, all soccer players are named Sam? _____
   Therefore, Sam is brave? _____

3. All girls are nice.
   All nice people are likable.
   Can you conclude:
   Therefore, all girls are likable? _____
   Therefore, all people who are likable are nice? _____
   Therefore, all nice people are girls? _____

4. All roses are flowers.
   All flowers have petals.
   Can you conclude:
   Therefore, all things with petals are flowers? _____
   Therefore, all roses have petals? _____
   Therefore, all flowers are roses? _____

5. No mammals can fly.
   Cows are mammals.
   Can you conclude:
   Therefore, all mammals are cows? _____
   Therefore, nothing that flies is a mammal? _____
   Therefore, cows cannot fly? _____

Introducing If-Then

Name_____

An **if-then sentence** is a statement with two parts—a *condition* and a *result.* The first part of the sentence contains the word "if" followed by a condition. The second part of the sentence contains the word "then" followed by the second happening. The two events in the statement are linked together so that if the first event or condition happens, then the second happening will also take place.

Example:
If the flying saucer lands, (condition) then I will be scared to death! (result)

If the condition part of the statement is met, you can conclude the result will happen.
Therefore, if you know it is true that the saucer will land, you can conclude that I will be scared to death!

But you cannot reverse an if-then statement.

If you know it is true that I am scared to death, you can not conclude that the flying saucer landed. I may be scared because of other happenings.

Here are some **if-then statements.** Read each statement and answer the question that follows.

1. If it rains, then I will get wet.
   It is raining.
   Can you conclude I got wet? _____

2. If it rains, then I will get wet.
   I am wet.
   Can you conclude it rained? _____

3. If the sun shines, then it will be hot.
   The sun is shining.
   Can you conclude that it is hot? _____

39

Iffy Situations

Name_____

Read these **if-then statements** carefully. Then decide if the conclusion is correct. If it is, write "yes." If it is not correct, write "no."

1. If Bob reads 10 books, then he will be awarded a reading certificate.
   Bob read 10 books.
   Can you conclude Bob was awarded a reading certificate? _____

2. If Jane watches TV, then she will not get her homework done.
   Jane did not finish her homework.
   Can you conclude Jane watched TV? _____

3. If Grandmother comes to visit, then Sara will sleep on the couch.
   Sara slept on the couch.
   Can you conclude Grandmother came to visit? _____

4. If Jim cuts the neighbor's grass, then he will earn $5.00.
   Jim cut the neighbor's grass.
   Can you conclude he earned $5.00? _____

5. If I stick a pin in my balloon, then it will pop.
   My balloon popped.
   Can you conclude I stuck a pin in it? _____

6. If Steve wins the race, then he will have three blue ribbons.
   Steve won the race.
   Can you conclude he has three blue ribbons? _____

7. If someone comes to my door, my dog barks.
   My dog is barking.
   Can you conclude there is someone at the door? _____

8. If it is Monday, then we have to go to school.
   We have to go to school.
   Can you conclude that it is Monday? _____

40

Story Time

Bob, Sally, and Jimmy are all in the same classroom and help in the library. During library period, each of them reads a different story to a class of younger children. To find out which story each person reads, read the clues carefully.

1. Sally's story did not have a wolf in it.
2. Bob's story did not have a number in the title.

	Bob	Sally	Jimmy
The Three Bears			
Three Little Pigs			
Little Red Riding Hood			

41

The Dog Show

Name _____

It's time for the annual dog show. Joe entered his collie in a dog show along with Jane's poodle and Sara's dachshund. Joe, Jane, and Sara all won prizes. One person won first place, one won second place, and one won third place. Sort out the clues to find out who won which prize.

1. Both girls' dogs placed higher than Joe's dog.
2. Sara's dog did not win first place.

	first	second	third
Dachshund			
Poodle			
Collie			

Favorite Nursery Rhymes

Name_____

Alice, Betty, Carol, and Dana are discussing their favorite books and stories. Each girl has a favorite nursery rhyme—Little Miss Muffett, Little Bo Peep, Mary, Mary Quite Contrary, and Humpty Dumpty. After reading the clues can you tell which rhyme is each girl's favorite?

1. Betty's favorite nursery rhyme is about a "little" girl.
2. Dana's favorite rhyme does not have a girl in it.
3. Alice does not like rhymes that have the word "little" in them.
4. Carol does not like sheep.

	Alice	Betty	Carol	Dana
Little Bo Peep				
Little Miss Muffet				
Mary, Mary Quite Contrary				
Humpty Dumpty				

Perfect Pets

Name _____

Bob, Kathy, Tom, and Judy each have a pet. Their pets are a cat, a dog, a gerbil, and a canary. Read the clues and see if you can match each person with the correct pet.

1. Tom's pet lives in a cage.
2. The boy who owns the dog goes to school with the girl who owns the cat.
3. Kathy's pet is a great singer.

	cat	dog	gerbil	canary
Judy				
Tom				
Kathy				
Bob				

Baseball Game

Name_____

Four friends, Benjamin, Ryan, Mark, and Stephen, all play baseball. Each boy is on a different team. One plays for the Cardinals, one for the Bears, one for the Eagles, and one for the Giants. The clues will help you match each boy with his baseball team.

1. Benjamin lives next door to the Eagles' catcher and a block away from Mark.

2. Ryan's team beat Mark's team and the Bears last week.

3. Benjamin's best friend plays on the Giants' team.

4. Last week Stephen's team beat Mark's team, but lost to the Cardinals and the Eagles.

	Cardinals	Bears	Eagles	Giants
Ryan				
Benjamin				
Stephen				
Mark				

Clown Capers

Name_____

Bozo, Zippy, Peppy, and Pete are all clowns with the circus. Each one has a different act. One of them does an act on the high wire, one works with trained poodles, one has a pet monkey in his act, and one drives a funny car. Use the clues below to find out which clown does which act.

1. Pete does not work with animals.
2. Zippy's act is the most dangerous.
3. Bozo and the clown with the pet monkey are good friends.

	Bozo	Zippy	Peppy	Pete
funny cars				
pet monkey				
trained poodles				
high wire				

Baseball Cards

Name_____

Phil, Megan, Brian, Karen, and Tim all collect baseball cards. Each person has a different number of cards in his/her collection. The person with the most has 100 cards. The others have 95, 75, 64, and 50 cards. Use the clues to find out how many cards each child has collected.

1. Both girls have collected an even number of cards.

2. Brian collected more than both girls and Phil, but less than Tim.

3. Karen collected more than Megan.

	50 cards	64 cards	75 cards	95 cards	100 cards
Brian					
Megan					
Phil					
Tim					
Karen					

47

Birthdays

Name _____

Sharon, David, Judy, Paul, and Kathy are comparing their birthdays. They were all born in the same year but in different months. They find out that one person was born on February 14th, one on April 10th, one on June 23rd, one on August 21st, and one on December 21st. Use the clues below to find out when each child has his or her birthday.

1. The boy whose birthday is in June goes to school with the girl whose birthday is in April.
2. David's birthday is before Kathy's but after Paul's.
3. Everyone gets cards on Sharon's birthday.

	February 14	April 10	June 23	August 21	December 21
Kathy					
Paul					
Judy					
David					
Sharon					

48

Neighbors

Name_____

Bart, Brian, Gretchen, Amy, Scott, and Pam all live on the same block. They are, however, different ages. Their ages are 5, 6, 8, 9, and 12 years old. Using the clues, you should be able to match each child with the correct age.

1. Gretchen is two years older than Pam.

2. Amy lives next door to Pam and across the street from the 12-year old and Bart.

3. Bart is three years younger than Scott.

4. The 6-year old girl lives across the street from Scott.

5. Gretchen is older than Pam and Brian, but younger than Scott and Amy.

	5 years old	6 years old	8 years old	9 years old	11 years old	12 years old
Amy						
Gretchen						
Brian						
Bart						
Pam						
Scott						

Measuring Up

Kristy, Heather, Matt, Tony, Leslie, and Greg have just been measured by the school nurse. The nurse dropped their records, so all their measurements are mixed up. Their heights were 52 inches, 53 inches, 55 inches, 56 inches, 58 inches, and 59 inches. Using the clues, you should be able to unscramble the records and find out how tall each child is.

1. Greg is one inch taller than Tony.

2. Heather is two inches taller than Matt.

3. Leslie is taller than the other girls and Matt, but shorter than Greg and Tony.

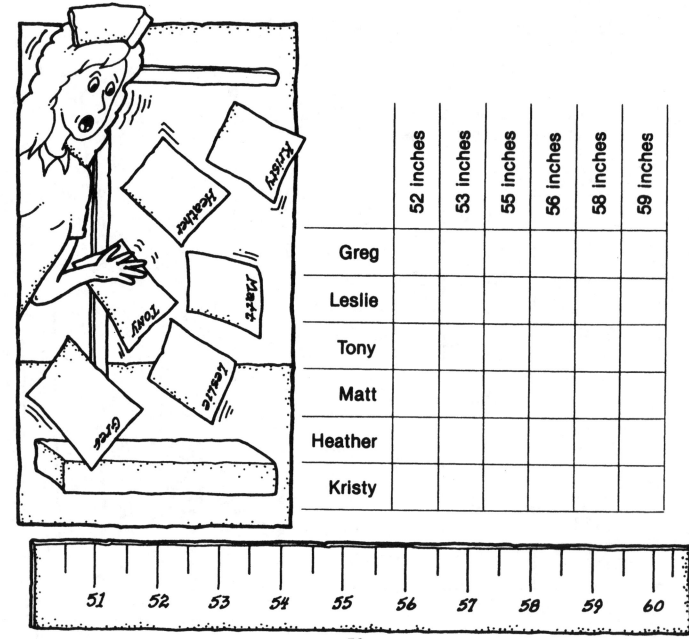

	52 inches	53 inches	55 inches	56 inches	58 inches	59 inches
Greg						
Leslie						
Tony						
Matt						
Heather						
Kristy						

50

Classmates

Name_____

David, Debbie, Sandra, and Alan all go to the same school, but they are in different classes. Their teachers' names are Ms. Stone, Mrs. Rock, Mrs. Land, and Mr. Waters. Their favorite subjects are math, reading, gym, and science. Use the clues below to match each student with his or her favorite subject and teacher.

1. The girl who likes math and the boy who likes science are not in Mr. Water's class.

2. Sandra, Alan, and the girl in Ms. Stone's class don't like gym.

3. The girl in Mrs. Land's class likes reading.

	science	gym	reading	math	Mrs. Rock	Mrs. Land	Mr. Waters	Ms. Stone
Alan								
Sandra								
Debbie								
David								
Mrs. Rock								
Mrs. Land								
Mr. Waters								
Ms. Stone								

Who's Who?

Name_____

Lucy, Barbara, Richard, and Erik are friends who live in the same neighborhood but on different streets. They live on Pine Street, Oak Street, 21st Avenue, and 25th Avenue. Each child has a different last name. Their last names are Ryan, Lang, Brown, and Evans. Use the clues below to match each first name with the correct last name and find which street each child lives on.

1. None of the children have the same first and last initial.

2. Ryan and his friend, Lucy, live on streets named after trees.

3. Evans, who lives on 21st Avenue, invited Richard and the girl who lives on Oak Street to her birthday party.

	Evans	Ryan	Lang	Brown	Pine Street	Oak Street	21st Avenue	25th Avenue
Erik								
Richard								
Barbara								
Lucy								
Pine Street								
Oak Street								
21st Avenue								
25th Avenue								

PINE STREET

OAK STREET

21st AVENUE

25TH AVENUE

Answers

Lesson 1 - Four of a Kind
1. dishes
2. meats
3. colors
4. drinks
5. birds
6. flowers
7. desserts
8. musical instruments
9. furniture
10. clothing
11. directions
12. states
13. silverware
14. storybook characters

Lesson 2 - Missing Links
1. basketball
2. John
3. saw
4. flashlight
5. flower
6. Chicago
7. Lori
8. scared
9. snow
10. frog
11. skip
12. mittens

Lesson 3 - Creating Relations
Answers will vary

Lesson 4 - Take It Out
1. canary, insects
2. skate, parts of bicycle
3. cherries, vegetables
4. kitten, wild animals
5. boat, have wheels
6. school, people
7. big, synonyms
8. belt, worn on the head
9. shovel, hand tools

Lesson 5 - Looking for Relations
Answers may vary but some possible answers are:
1. circles
2. triangles
3. even numbers
4. printed letters
5. even numbers
6. four-sided figures
7. vowels
8. round eyes or open eyes
9. curved lines

Lesson 6 - Curious Connections
1. feather
2. dog
3. book
4. fire
5. bone
6. blue
7. black
8. birth
9. ball

Lesson 7 - Being a Detective
1. blue
2. fly
3. ball
4. cow
5. right
6. bow
7. bed
8. plant
9. park

Lesson 8 - Cuing Into Characteristics
1. small
2. round
3. green
4. strong
5. night
6. turtle
7. rough
8. furry

Lesson 9 - Rhyming Analogies
1. yellow, bellow
2. frog, dog
3. fire, choir
4. white, light
5. sweet, parakeet
6. broke, croak

Lesson 10 - Picking Parts
1. bear
2. shoes
3. hand
4. leg
5. cookies
6. baseball diamond
7. roller skates
8. mouth
9. bricks
10. petal

Lesson 11 · Mainly Members
1. fruit
2. fish
3. chair
4. rocky road
5. Ben
6. dog
7. figures
8. Ohio
9. ham
10. animal
11. cereal
12. tree

Lesson 12 · Ready, Set, Action
1. fly
2. pound
3. hit
4. eat
5. tap
6. write
7. ride
8. run
9. learn
10. chirp

Lesson 13 · Similar or Opposite
1. night
2. small
3. tiny
4. sad
5. bad
6. low
7. scared
8. kitten
9. boy
10. cool

Lesson 14 · Analogies, Anyone?
1. attic
2. banquet
3. happy
4. clean
5. bake
6. coach
7. microscope
8. mammal
9. notes
10. hear
11. insect
12. book
13. porcupine,

Lesson 15 · Analogy Round Up
1. hammer
2. house
3. fly
4. cricket
5. land
6. club
7. paper
8. eat
9. scissors
10. cereal
11. bark
12. read
13. nervous
14. person
15. library

Lesson 16 · Creating Analogies
answers will vary

Lesson 17 · All Together
Example
1. has seeds
2. has seeds
3. yes

1. once was a puppy
2. is a is part of the alphabet
3. has four sides
4. is divisible by two
5. has wheels

Lesson 18 · Using All Statements
1. yes
2. six
3. yes
4. green
5. yes
6. yes
7. Mt. Washington needs teachers
8. Snickers is sweet
9. a grizzly has fur

Lesson 19 · Logic in Reverse
1. yes, no
2. yes, no
3. yes, no

Lesson 20 · Reversals in Review
1. no
2. no
3. no
4. no
5. yes, no
6. yes, no
7. no, yes
8. no, no, yes, yes, no

Lesson 21 - The Unstated All
1. yes
2. no
3. no
4. no
5. yes
6. no
7. yes, no
8. no, yes

Lesson 22 - Introducing No Statements
1. No, If one car was a bicycle, the statement would be false.
2. No, If one thing with wings was a car, the statement would be false.
3. No, If anything that swims was a car, the statement would be false.
4. are mammals
5. are rabbits
6. are dogs
7. glops are gleeks

Lesson 23 - Tricky Truths
1. true
2. true
3. true
4. false
5. true
6. false
7. false
8. false
9. true
10. answers will vary
11. answers will vary

Lesson 24 - No and Other Negatives
1. true
2. true
3. true
4. true
5. Things that fly don't have fur
6. Nothing that tastes good is green.
7. Things that are smart are not turkeys.

Lesson 25 - Put It In Reverse
1. false
2. true
3. false
4. true
5. true
6. false
7. true
8. false
9. false
10. true
11. false

Lesson 26 - Introducing Syllogisms
answers are included in instructions to students

Lesson 27 - Syllogism Sampling
1. valid
2. invalid
3. valid
4. valid
5. invalid
6. valid
7. valid
8. valid
9. valid
10. valid

Lesson 28 - Syllogism Scrimmage
1. yes, no, no
2. no, no, yes
3. yes, no, no
4. no, yes, no
5. no, yes, yes

Lesson 29 - Introducing If-Then
1. yes
2. no
3. yes

Lesson 30 - Iffy Situations
1. yes
2. no
3. no
4. yes
5. no
6. yes
7. no
8. no

Lesson 31 - Story Time
Bob - Red Riding Hood
Sally - The Three Bears
Jimmy - Three Little Pigs

Lesson 32 - The Dog Show
Collie - 3rd
Poodle - 1st
Dachshund - 2nd

Lesson 33 - Favorite Nursery Rhymes
Alice - Mary, Mary Quite Contrary
Betty - Little Bo Peep
Carol - Little Miss Muffet
Dana - Humpty Dumpty

Lesson 34 - Perfect Pets
Bob - dog
Kathy - canary
Tom - gerbil
Judy - cat

Lesson 35 - Baseball Game
Benjamin - Cardinals
Ryan - Eagles
Mark - Giants
Stephen - Bears

Lesson 36 - Clown Capers
Bozo - trained poodles
Zippy - high wire
Peppy - pet monkey
Pete - funny car

Lesson 37 - Baseball Cards
Phil - 75
Megan - 50
Brian - 95
Karen - 64
Tim - 100

Lesson 38 - Birthdays
Sharon - Feb. 14
David - Aug. 21
Judy - Apr. 10
Paul - June 23
Kathy - Dec. 21

Lesson 39 - Neighbors
Bart - 9
Brian - 5
Gretchen - 8
Amy - 11
Scott - 12
Pam - 6

Lesson 40 - Measuring Up
Kristy - 52"
Heather - 55"
Matt - 53"
Tony - 58"
Leslie - 56"
Greg - 59"

Lesson 41 - Classmates
David - Gym, Mr. Waters
Debbie - Math, Ms. Stone
Sandra - Reading, Mrs. Land
Alan - Science, Ms. Rock

Lesson 42 - Who's Who?
Lucy - Brown, Oak Street
Barbara - Evans, 21st Avenue
Richard - Lang, 25th Avenue
Erik - Ryan, Pine Street"